How to become a motorcycle instructor

by

David Harvey

All rights are reserved. No part of this publication may be reproduced, stored in a retrieval system or transmitted in any form or by any means, electronic, mechanical, photocopying, recording or otherwise, without the prior written permission of the author.

© David Harvey

March 2010 (first publication)

Revised January 2011

ISBN 978-1-4452-9018-8

Acknowledgements:

I would like to dedicate this modest tome to an ex-student of mine who went on to become a good friend and a wise counsellor and, amongst other things, encouraged me to do some writing. Thank you Paul Richardson, I shall always be very grateful to you.

My thanks must also go to those fellow motorcycle instructors who helped and encouraged me at the outset and continue to keep me on my toes. Most of them seem to be called 'Dave' - they know who they are.

Introduction:

When I decided to become a motorcycle instructor I was surprised at how little documentation there was available on this topic. There is a small but worthwhile collection of books about how to ride a motorcycle but nothing formally published on how to become a motorcycle instructor. Until something better comes along, this is my attempt to fill that small gap in the market. This book is aimed at potential and existing DSA (Driving Standards Agency) qualified motorcycle instructors in the UK.

Legislation and the training world does, of course, move on and when this book was first published in March 2010, the information it contained was current. It covers the two-part motorcycle test introduced in April 2009 but pre-dates the third EU driving licence directive due to become effective in January 2013. As with motorcycle riding in general and motorcycle instructing in particular, one is always looking to improve and learn new things and this publication is no different. Please feel free to send any corrections and suggestions direct to the author: <mail.904@googlemail.com> There is also a discussion group for motorcycle instructors in the UK: http://bit.ly/UKinstructors.

Contents:

Chapter 1	Why become a motorcycle instructor?
Chapter 2	What qualities are required?
Chapter 3	Get started
Chapter 4	Core competencies and teaching tips
Chapter 5	Instructor qualifications
Chapter 6	Cardington - my personal experience
Chapter 7	Cardington - some pointers
Chapter 8	CBT agenda
Chapter 9	CBT syllabus
Chapter 10	Direct Access Scheme (DAS)
Chapter 11	DAS and A2 lessons
Chapter 12	Practical test preparation
Chapter 13	Module one test manoeuvres
Chapter 14	Module two (road ride test)
Chapter 15	Post test instructing
Chapter 16	Driving Standards Agency
Chapter 17	Glossary
Chapter 18	Bibliography

Chapter 1

Why become a motorcycle instructor?

In two words, job satisfaction. If you enjoy riding a motorcycle and meeting people then provided you can communicate effectively, you can become a good motorcycle instructor. Natural enthusiasm will go a long way and will mean that the process of passing on your skills and knowledge can be enjoyable and satisfying for both instructor and student. This vocation offers plenty of fulfilment as the well-motivated student is learning a skill which they desire, plus you have the satisfaction of seeing a student develop their new-found skill.

You will, of course, be doing your bit for road safety by not only ensuring that the required knowledge and skills are in place but also instilling a good attitude in the student, something that is particularly important with riders under the age of 25. There is no denying that the consequences of getting it wrong on a motorcycle are potentially more serious than in a car and you have an opportunity to make a really worthwhile contribution to road safety.

Chapter 2

What qualities are required?

Patience is probably the most important attribute as, without it, a struggling student's fragile confidence and diminishing self-esteem will be undermined even further. You will need to like **meeting and dealing with a variety of people** from all walks of life. You almost have to be something of an **amateur psychologist** to help and encourage the student if they are becoming frustrated at their apparent inability to complete a particular task as will often happen on a machine control exercise.

Keeping calm in all situations is vital and sometimes **assertiveness** needs to be applied with certain students, particularly some younger ones who may be over-confident. You will need to be **persuasive** in the increasingly important area of improving rider attitudes. You must be able to **communicate effectively** and convey some of your **enthusiasm** for riding a motorcycle as this will help your training sessions to be both enjoyable and effective for yourself and your student.

A **positive mental attitude** is essential for both instructor and student but the instructor must lead by example. Your own motorcycle **riding skills** should, of course, be consistently reaching the very standards that you are encouraging your student to attain. This is particularly important as many students learn by watching something being done properly. Being able to ride a variety of machines to a smooth and consistent standard is quite helpful but being prepared to ride all year round in **all weathers** is necessary.

Flexibility is important as good instructors will adapt their approach and teaching techniques according to the student's needs and abilities. A good instructor must have an **open mind** and be receptive to new or alternatives ways of teaching and dealing with students as it is very easy to become stuck in a rut after a few years of instructing full time. **Tact** and a sense of humour often comes in handy when dealing with students, employers and fellow instructors.

Your knowledge of **motoring law** and the **Highway Code** should be above average. An up-to-date **general knowledge** of motorcycling matters is also helpful as the student will frequently look to the instructor for advice on clothing, machinery and accessories. Some very **basic maintenance skills** can come in handy so that you can carry out simple repairs to keep a machine roadworthy, skills such as adjusting a drive chain and replacing bulbs and control levers. Some simple **first aid** skills could be useful.

Your **personal appearance** and that of your riding kit and your motorcycle must be of a smart standard to reflect professionalism. You are an ambassador for not just the training industry but for motorcycling in general and an advert for your training school in particular.

Chapter 3

Get started

There are two basic routes to become a motorcycle instructor: pay a fee to a motorcycle training school providing an intensive (a week or so) instructor training course or find a good, local school and attach yourself to them. You might come to an arrangement whereby you go along one day a week (probably at the weekend) and over a few months you will hopefully develop and practice the necessary skills, ideally being mentored by an experienced instructor.

The usual idea is that in exchange for learning a new trade, in return you provide some free labour for the school. This latter method may also allow you to observe other instructors in action, in particular, seeing how a wide range of students and situations are developed.

Intensive courses will obviously be quicker and should be more focused upon you as a client. A good school will give you sufficient opportunity to practise your instructing skills upon 'real' students in addition to role play. Once you become a motorcycle instructor I recommend joining the Driving Instructors Association for various benefits such as individual public liability insurance.

Chapter 4

Core competencies and teaching tips

A motorcycle instructor needs to be able to spot faults and weaknesses in a rider, understand what is causing them and then implement an effective solution. Very straightforward when written down like that but these crucial skills take a while to develop and you will need the help and support of an experienced instructor. Once you have these core skills in place, you will benefit from observing and working with more experienced instructors as you can then 'cherry pick' techniques and styles to suit yourself after you have considered what appears to be most effective.

The student's needs: When first meeting a student it is important to put them at their ease, create a rapport and avoid making any pre-judgements. Ask plenty of 'open' questions to establish their previous experience, motivations and future motorcycling plans. At the beginning of each course (and new day) discuss your plans with the student and what your objectives are. At the end of each day summarise the achievements, emphasising the objectives met. It may be necessary to be flexible in your methods and approach, adapting them to the student. A good relationship needs to be developed as soon as possible so that the student feels that they can discuss their fears and anxieties, thereby enabling you to address them appropriately. They should feel sufficiently comfortable with the instructor so that they can admit to their mistakes and not feel intimated by their own perceived lack of skill. To help build confidence, make sure that you only ask them to do tasks which you believe they have a good chance of achieving. There must not be any bad or offensive language or unnecessary physical contact. Show respect to your students and colleagues in the hope that it will be reciprocated. Keeping some sort of training log book is a good idea, especially if the student does not have the same instructor each day. Make sure there are sufficient breaks bearing in mind tiredness on the student's part and the effects of the weather, particularly as the student may not have the best motorcycle clothing. You may be used to spending all day on a motorcycle but your student will not!

Motivation: The student obviously has some motivation simply by signing up for a course but this motivation may have to be reinforced if the student becomes discouraged with a temporary halt in the learning progress (sometimes called a 'learning plateau'). This can be done by taking a close interest in, and drawing attention to, even the smallest areas of progress. This may require the breaking down of a lesson or manoeuvre into smaller, more manageable steps where good progress is more obvious to the student.

Planning: This is very important so that tasks are set for the pupil which are understandable and achievable. Be prepared to adapt those plans depending upon how the student fares. You will need to make an initial assessment of your student's ability so that you can plan appropriately. Quite often a student may struggle to achieve a certain skill despite much effort and perseverance. In that situation it can often help to work on a completely different topic and come back to the troublesome one later. Different students will learn at different rates. The aims and objectives of each course and session should be explained at the outset and summarised (using Q and A) at the conclusion. The aims of a session tend to be of a general nature e.g. 'we are going to learn about and practise emergency stops'. The objectives will include the student's understanding and use of the motorcycle controls and the correct order and degree of application.

Praise: When praising a student for their riding give specific instances of why you are pleased so that your praise is based upon facts which they can verify for themselves. e.g. instead of saying 'That was a very good U-turn', say instead: 'That was a very good U-turn because you kept the engine revs at just the right level all the way through the turn'. Better still, ask them why they think it went well. Avoid exaggerated praise as this will appear insincere.

'Questions and Answers': Q and A is always an important technique for establishing the experience and knowledge of a student as well as holding the attention of a group. You can also use Q and A to help in the student's learning process. Make an effort to learn all of the students' names and use them regularly. Make frequent eye-contact with all students on an equal basis so that no one feels left out and no one particular student is hogging your attention. Try to ensure that your questions are equally spread amongst all of the students. If a student is struggling with a particular exercise, ask them which aspect they find difficult and why. Rather than hand them the solution 'on a plate' use Q and A to steer the student towards the solution so that they feel as if they have solved the problem themselves. The student will achieve more satisfaction this way and as a consequence they are more likely to retain and deploy their newly-found skill.

Methods of learning: 'What I hear I forget; what I see, I remember; what I do, I understand.

Learning by repetition (rote): This is the lowest form of learning as it involves the memorising of particular facts or actions without necessarily understanding their relevance. An element of rote learning cannot be avoided and is useful for remembering certain facts such as stopping distances. Learning by understanding (Gestalt) involves being able to attach meaning to information. Use diagrams to help explain a point, as a picture is worth a thousand words. Transfer of learning: Use previous experience as a cyclist, pedestrian or car driver to assist in their motorcycling skills.

Explain, Demonstrate and Practise (EDP):

Explain what is involved in the exercise and why it is important. You should also explain when, where and how it should be carried out. The demonstration should show what is required without showing off and making the exercise appear more difficult than it really is. The student needs to feel that they can reach a similar standard with a little practice. The demonstration should emphasise the individual skill components of the exercise. I don't recommend demonstrating how something should NOT be done in case that makes a stronger impression than the correct demonstration. I have seen this happen. Conclude by dispelling any apprehension the students may have. When the student starts to practise give plenty of initial guidance so that the student achieves early success.

Important points to remember about learning:

- Establish what the student already knows and build upon this.
- Structure the learning in small, manageable steps and goals.
- Be consistent with instructions and terminology and ensure that they are understood.
- Keep explanations short and simple, emphasising key points.
- Make sure instructions are 'positive' i.e. tell them what to do, not what not to do.
- Explain the purpose of a demonstration before giving it.
- Adjust your demonstration to the correct level of the student (i.e. don't show off).
- Allow the learner plenty of practice and be aware of the value of occasionally leaving the student alone (i.e. supervised at a safe distance) to practise.
- Try to ensure that initial practice is successful as failure will discourage.
- Justified praise and continuous feedback will stimulate progress and boost self-confidence.
- Early positive reinforcement will prevent bad habits becoming established.
- Avoid comparing one student with another.
- Empathise with a student who is struggling and reassure them that periods of slow learning are normal.
- Older students may take longer to develop certain practical (psychomotor) skills.

- Fear of failure is a prime cause of anxiety.
- Be prepared to vary instruction methods.
- Avoid expanding on variables before a student has grasped the basics.
- Aims of a motorcycle training course:
- To develop safe attitudes and behaviour to enable students to:
- Recognise situations where accidents are more likely to occur.
- Identify the causes of accidents.
- Be aware of their own limitations and abilities.
- Apply defensive driving with a view to minimising the risk of becoming involved in an accident.

General tips:

- Remember to gather all students around you so that they can see and hear you.
- Use easy-to-follow diagrams to help your teaching.
- Have teaching aids readily to hand before starting the session.
- Hi-viz vests are to be worn and headlights should be on dipped beam.
- Use regular Q and A with students to maintain their interest and establish the extent of their existing knowledge.
- Ask them to turn off the ignition with their left hand, thus ensuring that they have selected neutral.
- Refer regularly to notes. Use them as a check list.
- If you are asked a question to which you do not have the answer then say so straight away rather than trying to bluff your way through. Tell the questioner that you will find out and get back to them.

- At the end of each session, if there is another instructor observing or assisting, ask them if there is anything they would like to add. This will appear more professional than asking your colleague: 'Have I forgotten anything?'

Chapter 5

Instructor qualifications

To be eligible, the DSA has a number of requirements;

- Be aged 21 or over.
- Hold a current full GB or Northern Ireland driving licence.
- Have held full motorcycle entitlement for at least three years. (Automatic or A1 categories are insufficient).
- They must also be considered a 'fit and proper' person. In very simple terms it would help if the applicant was free of any motoring or criminal convictions.

Make sure you ask your school for access to their copy of the ATB (Approved Training Body) manual so that you can study and understand its contents, as both the instructor and the school must adhere to its requirements at all times. The manual will give full details of the application requirements. The DSA issues bulletins from time to time so make sure that you are shown those as well.

In terms of teaching riders to ride on the roads, the DSA has three levels of progressively-certified instructors;

1. Down-trained - this is the first step where the training school trains the instructor 'in-house'. Once the DSA approves the application a photocard-style certificate is issued, known as a 'CBT1'.

2. Cardington qualified - this is the second step where the holder of a CBT1 card/certificate has successfully passed a two day assessment at the DSA's centre for training and assessment in Cardington, Bedfordshire. Proof of this is in the form of a CBT1C card/certificate being issued. There are two aspects to this middle qualification. Firstly, it proves that you know what you are talking about when teaching CBT (Compulsory Basic Training) and secondly, you are also now qualified to down-train and supervise new instructors coming in at level 1.

3. Direct access qualified - passing a half day assessment at Cardington allows the holder of a CBT1D card to additionally supervise students on large (more than 47 bhp) motorcycles.

All instructors must carry their instructor identity cards with them when instructing.

Chapter 6
Cardington - my personal experience

To earn your CBT1C card you must attend Cardington for an assessment of your skills over a two day period. This is quite demanding as all that you say and do is under the scrutiny of experienced assessors as well as fellow candidates. Having been a down-trained CBT instructor since May 2003, I decided to attend the Cardington assessment course in September 2003. The courses run from Monday to Tuesday or Wednesday to Thursday, starting at 8.30am and finishing at 5pm. There is a one-hour lunch break and short mid-morning and mid-afternoon tea breaks. The two days are quite demanding and it is a good idea to stay overnight the day before the course starts so that you are fresh from the outset.

The Driving Standards Agency site at Cardington covers a large area, the main features of which are two enormous aircraft hanger-like buildings where airships (such as the R101) were built. It is easy to find. There is a large area of tarmac (called the 'pad') sufficient for the movement of HGVs etc. and it is compulsory that safety vests are worn anywhere on the pad, both as a pedestrian and as a rider. There is, of course, plenty of room to conduct practical on-site riding.

By the time of my attendance, I had conducted about 40 CBTs and I felt quite comfortable with them, but having to conduct elements of the CBT course at Cardington under the scrutiny of a DSA assessor and fellow candidates is something else. At the very beginning of the course the assessor checked and retained our CBT instructor cards and emphasised that he would only give them back at the end of the course if he was satisfied with our performance! You are aware also that your fellow candidate is required to scrutinise your performance very closely as their performance in a supervisory role is being assessed as well.

Each course is run by one DSA assessor who is allocated three candidates, although on my course one of the candidates failed to show up, without letting anyone know. This was a bad idea as it would count as a 'fail' and if you have two 'fails' you have to wait twelve months for a third attempt. For most of the time the assessor will play the role of a student who is taught certain CBT exercises by one candidate whilst the remaining candidates act as supervisors. Once the candidate has finished the exercise, he/she must be debriefed by the supervisors in turn and they must start out by giving a decision as to whether or not the lesson delivered fulfilled the objectives. They will then go on to explain any criticisms they may have and give remedies and alternative solutions. The candidates will swap roles frequently between 'instructor' and 'supervisor' and they may also be asked to play out the role of a student under instruction by the assessor with the other candidates 'supervising' and debriefing the assessor.

Although the course lasts two days, the candidates do not actually teach an entire CBT course, merely extracts. On my course, there were no interim debriefings by the assessor on the various exercises. For sessions on the training pad, it is very likely that you will be required to work within an area 30 feet by 80 feet which is the smallest size allowed for a CBT site. Teaching junction work in such a small area will require some thought and planning and ideally, some prior practice.

The assessor spent plenty of time at the very outset outlining what the procedure was and what he expected. He stressed that when in the supervising role it is vital to be brutally honest with the fellow instructor in addressing any areas where you are dissatisfied with their performance. You must treat the fellow instructor as your employee upon whose shoulders the high standards of your training organisation rests. If your instructor's work is poor then it will be your own school's reputation at risk.

Marking System - For each exercise you teach or supervise, there are four grades: 1 and 2 are unsatisfactory, 3 and 4 are satisfactory. You are marked separately in the two roles of 'instructor' and 'supervisor'.

Road Ride - Each candidate was required to act as an instructor on a road ride which on my course included u-turns, emergency stops and hill starts and lasted for almost an hour. The DSA supplied radios. There is an internal road system (including a roundabout) marked out within the centre so do not assume that the road ride only starts once you leave the centre's gates. Instead, assume that it starts immediately from the 'pad'. I was warned beforehand that the quality of my machine control would be under scrutiny by both the assessor and my fellow candidate and also by any other DSA employees who may have seen me riding on or around the site.

Chapter 7

Cardington - some pointers

The assessor will go into 'role' after first giving you some basic information about his character's age and experience. Be sure to use plenty of Q and A for additional detail just as you would on a conventional CBT. One of the important skills you must display is that of having sufficient control of the student. A prime example of this might arise on an exercise where the 'student' has to be taught how to pull away in a straight line and then stop safely at a precise point.

During the road ride, the assessor will play the role of a student under your direction and he will deliberately introduce a few errors, which he will expect you to note and correct at frequent roadside debriefings, which the assessor will convene. He will probably keep on repeating those same errors until you correct them. One candidate will be acting as a supervisor and they will be able to hear the fellow candidate's instructions for subsequent debriefing. The supervisor must also observe the fellow candidate's quality of machine control and road positioning so as to keep the student safe.

It is not necessary for the candidate to know the road ride route as the assessor will use hand or indicator signals as an invitation for the candidate to give directions over the radio. It is stressed that the radio instructions should be short and unambiguous. i.e. *'Follow the road straight ahead at the roundabout'* and NOT: *'Go straight over the roundabout.'* During the 'on-road' element, consider the other trainee behind you as an independent road user and indicate accordingly. The Cardington assessor is happy for you to be closer than the 'two second rule' at less than 30mph as long as you are NOT directly in line behind him. At speeds above 30mph revert to the two second gap with offset. At 'Stop' and 'Give Way' lines it is OK to move partially alongside but without blocking the student's view into the main road. The instructor must be satisfied that it is safe for the student to move. Once again,

21

the instructor must demonstrate adequate control of the student. When the assessor is setting off from rest or carrying out a lifesaver, ensure that you are positioned so as not to obstruct their view.

When pulling over for a debrief, remember not to pull in too close behind the student's machine when stopping as you need to ensure that when the student pulls away, his view of the road behind is not blocked. If necessary, stop ahead of the student, giving them plenty of room. When 'debriefing' the student identify the shortfall, explain (with diagrams) and consider demonstrating how it should be done. Always give a remedy.

Radio work: When you are happy with the student's progress, back off a little but be prepared to take control again if they start to make mistakes. When riding around get the assessor looking into the distance, namely, forward observations and planning. They do not want retrospective instruction (what they should have done back there, etc.) Save that for a debrief. Remember to reinforce OSM PSL on approach, so start early. Do not simply point out hazards. The student needs to be told what to do and when to do it in sufficient time.

As is very common among instructors I have a flip-up front full-face helmet. My assessor told me that when demonstrating on the Cardington pad, I should ride with the front down but it is OK to have the visor fully raised. Do not sit astride a machine without wearing a helmet. If some of these procedures seem a little over-cautious, it is because the DSA places a very high priority on keeping the student as safe as possible under all circumstances.

When debriefing in your role as a supervisor ask the instructor:

- how they thought it went
- has learning taken place?
- was the object of the lesson achieved?

- how would they do it differently next time?

When being debriefed by a fellow candidate be open-minded when alternative ideas are suggested but also be prepared to explain and justify a particular point of view. You may want to explain why you teach a certain topic in a particular way.

Conclusions:

There is no substitute for experience combined with thorough preparation. Something like six months practice as a down-trained instructor seems to be a good idea before going to Cardington. It is important to be knowledgeable, decisive and assertive.

It is OK to refer to notes during the course and I recommend this to ensure that you do not miss out any essential points in the heat of the moment. You are not expected to do all of your teaching entirely from memory. Consider preparing some check lists so that nothing important is missed in a session. Bear in mind that the assessor will not be impressed if you deliver your talks by reading out from your notes word for word, parrot-fashion.

Remember that the DSA wishes to maintain high and consistent standards and that it likes all of the various lessons and exercises to be self-contained with minimal overlap or going off topic. Make sure that you are familiar with all of the DSA's motorcycle publications and their contents.

Chapter 8

CBT agenda

All learners on mopeds and motorcycles must satisfactorily complete a CBT course before riding on the road. In addition, with effect from February 1st 2001, all new holders of full car licences must complete CBT if they wish to take advantage of their moped entitlement. Before the CBT course can start, each student must show both the photocard and paper counterparts of their UK driving licence so that the correct provisional entitlement can be seen to be in force as well as proving their identity. The instructor must also check the counterpart to ensure that the student is not banned from riding at the time of the training!

Once the entire CBT course has been completed to the satisfaction of the instructor then a DL196 certificate will be issued to the student. The certificate is only valid for two years. If both theory and practical tests have not been passed within this time, CBT will have to be re-taken. Where a DL196 certificate is validating the moped entitlement on a full car licence then there is no expiry date.

Here is an outline of a CBT session. It usually takes a full day for most students but for some students it can take an extra day or two to reach the required standard. CBT is broken down into five elements which must be covered in the following order:

Element A:

- Aims of CBT
- Content of CBT
- Equipment and clothing
- Check licences and eyesight

Element B:

- Motorcycles and their controls
- Basic safety checks and use of the stands
- Wheeling the motorcycle and braking to a stop
- Starting and stopping the engine

Element C:

- Riding in a straight line and stopping
- Riding slowly
- Using the brakes
- Changing gear
- Riding a figure-of-eight
- Emergency stopping
- Rear observation and blind spot demonstration
- Turning left and right
- U-turn

Element D:

- Conspicuity
- Legal requirements
- Vulnerability
- Speed
- Highway Code
- Anticipation
- Rear observations
- Road positioning
- Separation distance
- Weather conditions
- Road surfaces
- Alcohol and drugs
- Attitude
- Hazard perception

Element E:

- Practical on-road riding

(A legally required minimum of two hours of tuition on public roads).

Chapter 9

CBT syllabus

This is the longest chapter and is intended to provide a detailed syllabus for a CBT session. The five elements must be taught in this order although there is flexibility about the order in which topics are taught within each element. Elements A and B often take up to 45 minutes each. Any longer than that and you may have difficulty in holding everyone's attention.

Element A:

CBT is a legally required course introduced on December 1st 1990 to teach basic skills to new riders with the following aims:

- To reduce the high level of accidents involving inexperienced riders.
- To improve rider safety and machine control.
- To increase rider awareness and good practice.

Content: CBT is not a test but a continuous assessment. There are five elements to CBT that must be taken in the following sequence:

Element A:	Introduction
Element B:	Practical on-site training
Element C:	On-site riding
Element D:	Practical on-road training
Element E:	On-road riding

CBT is compulsory for all new motorcyclists and for new car drivers wanting moped entitlement. The learner may not ride unaccompanied until CBT is satisfactorily completed. The instructor to student maximum ratio is 1:4 on site, 1:2 on-road. Upon successful completion a DL196 certificate is issued to the rider which is valid for two years. This is an important document forming part of the driving licence and needs to be kept safe. It entitles the holder to practise their riding on public roads as a 'learner', unsupervised. They must display 'L' plates and ride a machine no bigger than 125cc, assuming they are aged 17 or older. Pillion-carrying and riding on motorways are prohibited. If the holder is aged 16 then they are restricted to a moped.

Equipment and Clothing:

Without it, we are more vulnerable to injuries and we can become cold and wet which can cause a loss of concentration, adverse reaction times and possibly a lack of movement and feel for the controls.

Safety Helmet:

Always buy brand new as it is a single use safety item. It is only designed to take one impact, therefore do not borrow one or buy a used one. It is the only item of legally required clothing and it must also be correctly fastened. It must carry a BSI 6658:1985 kite mark* (prior to July 2000) or UNECEC 22.05# white label with an E number in a circle (post July 2000). '04' or '03' are illegal in the UK. From July 1st 2000, it has been legal to wear a helmet purchased anywhere within the EU provided it carries CE mark: EC22/05.

The testing procedures cover impact protection, penetration resistance, basic design, chin strap security, chin bar strength and resistance to solvents and temperature extremes.

 # Does not test for chin bar strength or penetration and is generally believed to be less exhaustive than the BSI test.

An ACU gold sticker means that the helmet is considered to be safe for competition use by the ACU (Auto Cycle Union).

Fastener types: quick release (seat belt), double 'D'-ring, bar and buckle, and ratchet.

Safety helmets come in three styles;

Full face: comes with hinged visor. It protects the face and jaw and gives the most weather protection. It is quieter and hotter than the open face type and it is not so easy to talk whilst being worn. The wearing of glasses can be a problem.

Open face: (jet style) is usually the cheapest and noisiest, with reduced protection from frontal impact and the weather.

Hybrid: (hinged or flip-up front) is usually more expensive and slightly heavier but very convenient as it enables talking without removal. It must be shut down whilst on the move.

Helmet materials: The hard outer shell can be made of the following materials;

Polycarbonate: A type of plastic which tends to be cheaper and lighter in weight than other materials. Contact with paint, stickers, solvent and fuel should be avoided as this can weaken the shell. It will have an average life span of approximately three years.

Fibre glass: Is usually heavier than polycarbonate and is not affected by solvents or stickers. It will have an average life span of approximately five years.

Kevlar or carbon fibre laminate: This material is the lightest, strongest and most expensive.

Helmet fit and care:

Try on a wide range to find a firm and snug fit all over the head with no localised pressure points. For this reason, buying by mail order is not very convenient. Any movement should be in the scalp itself.

- New helmets will 'bed-in' to the owner's head shape.
- Show the student how to put one on by holding both straps and prising apart.
- The helmet must not be loose and also check the fit with the strap correctly fastened with two finger's worth of slack.
- Make sure that the rider's glasses can fit inside a full-face helmet comfortably.
- Any Velcro fastenings are not the main method of fastening.
- Take care not to drop the helmet or leave it balanced precariously anywhere.

Visors and goggles:

Eye protection, whilst not required by law, is essential and must fit over your normal glasses if required. Visors and goggles used must carry the BS 4110 kite mark which covers light transmission, resistance to scratching ('A') and impacts. Alternatively, UNECE Regulation 22.05 (It will be marked with a UN 'E' mark and the first two digits of the approval number will be '05'). If the rider wears spectacles then the lenses should be made of plastic and not glass.

'X' is the lowest grade impact protection, 'Y' medium and 'Z' the highest.

Goggles should have a BS marking for safety glass. Don't wear tinted visors during darkness or poor visibility. Clean with warm, soapy water and a soft cloth to maintain good visibility at all times. Do not wipe with a dry cloth or glove as this will cause scratching and a 'starring' effect at night. Visors can be bought separately and should be replaced when they become scratched. Keep the inside of the visor clean and polished to minimise fogging. A clean outer surface will encourage water to 'fling off'.

Clothing Materials:

Leather: Only buy purpose-made motorcycle clothing rather than 'fashion' leather items. Motorcycle leathers will be of the optimum thickness and grade of leather correctly stitched to resist tearing. Leathers should be a snug fit and as a result, there is not much room for additional layers. Leathers have good abrasion resistance, the thicker and heavier grade the better. There may be double thickness panels and body armour in vulnerable areas such as elbows, shoulders, hips, knees and back. Leather can be hot in summer and cold in winter and is not fully waterproof. If it gets wet it needs to be allowed to dry out slowly and may need to be treated.

Man-made: Plastic/PVC/Nylon/textile materials are cheaper and lighter in weight and more flexible but they can be sweaty and can melt on a hot exhaust pipe. Such items are designed to fit over normal 'day' clothes so when trying on, make sure that there is sufficient room and no constrictions. Poor abrasion resistance and friction temperature can cause nylon to melt onto skin. Modern textile clothing is much better as it can offer good abrasion resistance, waterproof membrane and built-in body armour and is easier to wash. Alternatives include heavy duty denim, especially if it includes special abrasion-resistant fibres.

One-piece: Mostly leather, has the advantage that the jacket will not ride up creating a gap that can leave the rider prone to draughts and abrasion injury.

Two-piece: Can be leather or man-made materials and ideally they will zip together. It has the convenience of allowing the two items to be bought separately according to budget and sizing.

Gloves: Purpose-made motorcycle gloves must be worn, as they will have the necessary strengthening panels and be of the right material for resisting abrasion. They are usually made of leather but can also be of textile construction, or a combination of both. Fingers and hands need to be kept as warm as possible without compromising feel for the controls. For long winter journeys consider handlebar covers and/or heated grips. Regarding the latter, obtain expert advice to ensure that your machine has sufficient electrical capacity for such an accessory.

Boots: Until purpose-made motorcycle boots can be afforded then strong leather footwear will do, ideally with ankle and shin protection combined with a stiff sole to prevent crushing injuries. Industrial work wear or hiking boots could be worn provided they allow sufficient use of foot controls. Watch out for loose laces becoming entangled on foot controls. Be wary of steel toecaps as in an accident they can cut into the toes.

Safety warning - Understand the dangers of riding:

- Without eye protection or adequate gloves.
- With scratched, damaged or tinted visors or goggles.
- With a damaged helmet.
- Wearing shorts, tee shirt, sandals or trainers.
- Without adequate clothing in bad weather.

Conclusion:

Buy the best you can afford and look after it and it will last for many years.

For restricted budgets, consider second hand, purpose-made jackets and trousers where any damage or wear is obvious.

Do not buy or borrow a second hand safety helmet.

Motorcycling will be safer and more enjoyable if you are warm, dry, comfortable and in control.

Check licences and eyesight:

Read a car (not motorcycle) number plate at 20.5 metres (67 feet or 25 paces) in good daylight with the aid of glasses or contact lenses if normally worn in which case they must be worn during the course. The letters and figures to be 79.4 mm (3.1 inches) high. If the eyesight test is failed, the course cannot continue.

Element B - Motorcycles and their controls:

Controls:

Adopt a logical sequence so that nothing is missed. e.g. start at left hand switchgear and work your way around clockwise. Finish by explaining the use of clutch and gears. Include fuel, reserve, choke and accelerator, emphasising the importance of smooth and progressive use of all of the controls.

Hand Controls:

- clutch lever
- lighting switches (dipped beam on-road)
- indicator usage (use without looking down)
- horn (check purpose of)
- ignition on/off
- accelerator demonstration
- front brake lever (four fingers) and stop light switch
- master cylinder reservoir
- electric starter button (release once engine is running)
- engine cut-off/kill switch (avoid using except in an emergency)
- carburettor and choke operation
- fuel tap positions and explain main and reserve supplies

Foot Controls:
- rear brake
- kick starter (use with bike on centre stand and fold back in after use)
- gear change lever (explain gear change procedure)
- Instruments:
- speedometer
- rev-counter
- warning lamps
- water, temperature and fuel gauges

Controls should be used smoothly and progressively and caressed gently without looking down at them. Clutch and brake levers have adjusters to compensate for wear and allow adjustment for comfort. Finish by explaining the use of clutch and gears even if all your students are on automatics.

Using the brakes:

Q and A: Explain the use and effects of front and rear braking (only when upright). Explain skid correction and wet road stopping distances.

Basic safety checks and use of the stands:

Why? To reduce our vulnerability and to ensure the proper operation of the motorcycle.

Brakes: Check for any fraying cables which should be correctly adjusted, and the brake wear indicators. Cable operation should be smooth. If not, lubrication or replacement may be required. On hydraulic systems, check the reservoir level.

Oils and fluids: Check levels with a dipstick or sight glass whilst the machine is on level ground. Also the battery, coolant and hydraulic reservoirs will need to be checked.

Lights and electrics: Check all electrics, lights, horn and emergency cut out/kill switch. Check the security of the plug lead.

Tyres and wheels: The legal requirement for motorcycle tyre tread depth is 1mm over three quarters of the central area around the entire circumference. For mopeds the requirement is merely visible tread over three quarters of the width around the entire circumference. Spin the wheels for trueness and soundness of spokes. Check the tyres for cuts and bulges. There should be no play in the wheel bearings. Explain the importance of correct tyre pressures.

Steering: Check the head bearings for smooth and free movement but not too much slack.

Suspension: Compress the front forks and mention oil seal leaks. Show rear suspension movement and pivot wear check.

Sprockets and chain: They are prone to wear and require routine inspection, adjustment and lubrication. Emphasise the importance of achieving correct tension and alignment.

Stands: They need to be secure and lubricated so that they swing out of the way. Don't sit on the bike whilst it is on its stand as this can place unnecessary wear on the stand.

Finally make sure that there are no loose items such as number plate, 'L' plates or fasteners. Mirrors, lights and reflectors should be clean and unbroken. Cleaning the bike on a regular basis will make it easier to spot any problems.

Daily checks: - P.O.W.D.E.R.Y.- (Petrol - Oil - Water - Damage - Electrics - Rubber - 'You').

Using the centre stand: The machine should be on firm, level ground. The bars should point straight ahead with the steering lock off, the right foot covering the centre stand lever and the left hand gripping the left handlebar.

Push down on the rear grab handle and then rock the machine forward off the stand, applying pressure with the right foot for extra security. Look straight head, not down. With both stand feet on the ground, transfer the right hand to apply the front brake with all four fingers. Make sure that the centre stand springs up and lean the machine slightly into the body.

To put the machine on the centre stand, apply the front brake with the right hand whilst gently pushing the centre stand downwards with the right foot until contact is made with the ground. Using feel, make sure that both of the metal centre stand feet are touching the ground and then transfer the right hand to a good hand hold at the rear of the machine. Next, ensure that the rider's weight is directly above the right foot with the ball of the foot now pressing on the centre stand lever. Use the body weight to act on the centre stand lever while at the same time pulling the machine upwards and to the rear to roll the machine on to the stand. Emphasise that technique is the key, not strength.

This procedure needs to be followed to minimise the risk of personal injury and machine damage. The instructor should stand opposite the student ready to catch the machine should it fall away from the student. Even if the machine does not have a side stand, you should explain how to use one.

Wheeling the motorcycle and braking to a stop:

(The DSA no longer requires the wearing of gloves and helmets for taking the bike off the stand or for wheeling the machine. This was explained as being more of a reflection of the real world as no one gets kitted up to wheel their bikes out of their garages. The DSA does require helmet and gloves to be worn any time the student sits on the bike). Wheel the machine forward using the front brake to stop in a straight line. (On scooters, the left handlebar lever can be used to operate the rear brake for improved stability). Look ahead to where you want to go, caressing the brake lever all the time using all four fingers. When the student practises this task, the instructor should be alongside the machine ready to catch it the first time each student makes a turn. Go straight ahead first, then left turn and right turn. Stop in a straight line. This should be done one student at a time.

Avoid:
- holding somewhere other than the handlebar grips
- wobbling insecure control
- looking down
- harsh use of the front brake
- knocking of shins on footrests

Starting and stopping the engine:

With the bike off its stand the student should sit astride the machine wearing helmet, vests and gloves. Explain FIGS (Fuel, Ignition, Gears and Starter) starting procedure.

Fuel: Make sure there is enough for the journey and that the tap is switched on. Switch off choke fully as soon as engine runs smoothly without it.

Ignition: Switch on with the left hand, making sure the cut-off/kill switch is on. Always use the main ignition switch to switch off the engine. Using the kill switch but leaving the ignition on will run down the battery and possibly damage the ignition system.

Gears: Make sure the neutral light is on. Move the bike forward to double check. Explain what a false neutral is.

Starter: Use the electric start in preference to any kick-starter and release the button as soon as the engine is running.

Safety position: The left foot should be on the ground (even for scooter riders) as it keeps the right foot away from passing traffic. The clutch is pulled in, with the right foot applying the rear brake to hold the machine in place and illuminate the rear light which makes the machine more obvious in poor visibility. Turn off the ignition switch using the left hand. (This will ensure that neutral has been selected). Dismount and place on the centre stand correctly.

Conclude element 'B' by asking the student to switch the engine off. If they are in the habit of doing this with the left hand then this ensures that they have found neutral first.

Element (C)
Riding in a straight line and stopping at a defined point:

Helmet, gloves and vest on, FIGS. Explain the procedure for moving off using first gear. With the clutch in, tread gear lever down into first gear.

- safety position
- apply rear brake only
- steady accelerator - 'busy' tick over
- release clutch slowly - think - 'dimmer-switch'
- develop feel for biting point
- release rear brake smoothly

Stopping - easy as '**A B C**':
- **A**ccelerator closed smoothly
- **B**rake with both brakes (front first)
- **C**lutch in and left foot down as you come to a halt

Practise at least twice. At this very important stage where the novice is pulling away for the first few times, the instructor must have adequate control of the student and machine. I recommend that the instructor is alongside the student (to the left) with the instructor's left hand positioned ahead of the student's left hand ready to pull the clutch in should it be released too quickly. Consider positioning the cones in a diamond layout with the students proceeding clockwise. With the instructor positioned in the centre, this will allow a good view to check the order in which the brakes are being applied. For students with absolutely no prior experience, consider instructing the student to practise closing the accelerator and applying both brakes (in the correct sequence) whilst the instructor pushes the machine in neutral with a dead engine.

Riding slowly:

Explain why this is a necessary skill for junctions, heavy traffic, petrol stations, car parks and the like. The machine needs to be under full control at all times. The student must also be able to bring the machine to a controlled halt at a specific point (e.g.'Give Way' lines).

Demonstrate the safety position, having steady, busy engine revs, with the biting point engaged and the machine being held on the rear brake. Release the rear brake gently and re-apply to keep smooth motion at walking pace. Keep the head up, (not looking down at controls) look where you are going with arms relaxed and thighs gripping the fuel tank. Practise slow and minute changes in clutch lever position at the biting point, then 'ABC' to stop.

Practise: The instructor should be to the nearside of the student ready to pull in the clutch (one student at a time). After going straight ahead has been mastered, circle gently and slowly to left, then right.

Using the brakes:

Use both, to control speed and stop accurately at a pre-determined point. The student should practise stopping at simulated 'Give Way' lines.

- Avoid:
- stalling
- use of rear brake before front
- use of one brake only
- harsh and late use of brakes
- locking either wheel
- inaccurate stopping

Changing gear:

Explain:

- need for gears (e.g. bicycle)
- controls speed and affects fuel consumption
- higher gears have higher numbers
- hold up five fingers - sequential gearbox
- avoid block changing
- engage clutch between each change

Demonstrate: With the engine switched off, demonstrate the use of the accelerator, clutch and gear lever, emphasising the correct sequence and progressive use.

This process must be explained to riders of automatics even though they will not be riding a manual machine on CBT.

Tell the students that they should adjust their speed (using accelerator before brakes) for a given situation and once the speed is correct, select the correct gear for that speed.

Consider introducing early on in element C to allow them to practise in subsequent pad work, such as junctions or emergency stops.

Riding a figure-of-eight:

Explain: Low speed steering, balance and clutch control skills need to be practised to hopefully avoiding wobbling and putting feet down. The front brake is best avoided at such low speeds, especially when turning.

Demonstrate:
- head up, look where you want to go
- use back brake and clutch biting point
- steady accelerator in first gear
- may need knees slightly apart
- counter balance
- relaxed and flexible arms.

Practise:

Start with wide circles and gradually tighten.

Emergency stopping:

Q and A and give an explanation of the stopping procedure. Mention wet surfaces, skid correction and thinking distance.

Explain: How to stop safely in an emergency but under full control. Use the ABC principle, pulling the clutch in at the last moment and putting the left foot down. In an emergency there is no time for rear observation or gear changing.

Explain and show how the controls are to be used. Demonstrate the four-finger grip and emphasise that braking must be done in a straight line. Explain the principle of weight transfer and how, with the front brake doing most of the work, the rear of the machine becomes lighter. Only pull in the clutch as you come to a halt to maximise engine braking and minimise the possibility of the rear wheel skidding. With a dry surface the braking force applied should be approximately 75/25 (front/rear) and 50/50 in the wet.

Five steps:

1. accelerator closed
2. ease front brake on
3. ease rear brake on
4. squeeze front brake harder
5. clutch in and left foot down

Practise:

Stand to the offside of the bike to observe the operation of the brakes. Walk backwards and beckon the student forward with two gentle arm movements. Raise the right arm vertically and gently so as not to cause the student to snatch at the front brake. The instructor should check the application of the five steps in the correct order. There is usually no time for mirror checks or changing down through the gears once the stop signal has been given. Ensure that the student does not anticipate the stop signal: i.e. they should not close the accelerator until the arm signal has been given as the student's reaction time needs to be checked.

Faults:

Look out for anticipation, rear observation, late reaction, snatching at the controls, clutch in too early, one brake only in use, locked wheel, changing into a lower gear, stopping in neutral, forgetting to shut accelerator, accelerator coming back on slightly as the front brake is applied more fully or a stalled engine.

Rear Observation:

Explain:

Effective rear observations are required to be safe on the road especially when changing direction or speed. Do this by using the mirrors, lifesavers and a 180 degree turn of the head when stationary. Each type of observation has a different degree of head movement.

Demonstrate with the student on the bike wearing helmet and gloves, in the safety position with the engine switched off.

Mirrors:

They need to be checked and adjusted, warning that the glass may be convex to improve the angle of vision but that this can cause objects to appear further away than they really are. Mirrors, when regularly 'scanned', will give updates on the situation behind. Check the mirrors regularly when approaching hazards and before slowing. Demonstrate the blind spot danger.

Lifesaver:

The lifesaver is a 90 degree turn of the head to glance over the shoulder into the blind spot. This is usually done whilst the machine is on the move to check for a vehicle in the blind spot, just before the position of the motorcycle is changed significantly or where another vehicle may attempt to cross the motorcycle's path. e.g. junctions, roundabouts, overtaking and turning from a major road into a minor one.

Rear Observation over shoulder:

This involves a 180 degree turn of the head and upper body to be used just before pulling away from a stationary position. It should give sufficient time to evaluate the distance and speed of any approaching vehicles, with no blind spots. Revs and clutch biting point should be set before looking over the shoulder. Moving off should not start until the student is looking forward again.

Practise:

The student needs to understand which type of rear observation to carry out for a given situation and put that understanding into practise. Lifesavers should be done without causing the machine to wobble or veer off course and before the turn or change of position is executed.

Turning left and right (Junctions):

Define the 'dominant' (sometimes called the 'command') road position. Consider a whiteboard talk or walk the students through a simulated junction and consider using diagrams. The OSM (Observation, Signal, Manoeuvre) element is followed by PSL (Position, Speed and Look). Emphasise the cancelling of indicators. Lifesavers need to be used just before you turn right off a main road and one should be considered when turning left off a main road. When practising on the pad, ask students to stop at junctions as if a vehicle was approaching and after a while, ask them to keep moving (slowly) as if the road was clear.

U-turn:

Explain the practical use on the road and that it is a module one practical test manoeuvre. The machine should be under slow speed control with both feet on footrests once on the move. No signal is usually necessary but start with a 180 degree rear observation before moving off and then a lifesaver just before turning. Look out for hazards in both directions. As it is a slow speed manoeuvre, use of the front brake should be avoided.

Practise:

Long U-turn (180 degree rear observation, travel forward, lifesaver, then turn).

Short U-turn (optional): This variant is a little more difficult for the student who starts the turn as soon as the machine is under way following a 180 degree rear observation. It has the advantage that it can be executed in a smaller space and there is no need for a lifesaver.

Element D: (pre-ride classroom talk)

Conspicuity:
- Dipped headlights - must be used on all motorcycle training and testing, plus in conditions of poor visibility.
- Visibility aids - reflective stripes and stickers.
- Bright clothing - white helmet, Q and A about reflective and fluorescent clothing.
- Clean bike - to reflect light back at other road users.
- Road positioning: A motorcycle can be obscured behind a wide tree, or other traffic. Don't position yourself in other road user's blind spots. See and be seen - make yourself visible - slow down - anticipate.

Legal requirements for you and your machine:
- age 16/17
- driving licence with provisional motorcycle entitlement and DL196
- insurance - very important
- vehicle test certificate (MoT) if machine is three years old or more
- road fund licence (tax disc) to be displayed on the nearside
- 'L' plates of the correct size and displayed flat, front and rear
- roadworthy machine
- approved safety helmet correctly worn and fastened

Vulnerability:

Motorcyclists are part of a vulnerable group consisting of cyclists, horse riders and the infirm. The motorcyclist will come off worst in a collision with a larger vehicle irrespective of who is to blame. We are prone to injury even at very low speed which is why we wear the most protective clothing we can afford. We are not as protected from the weather conditions and therefore getting cold and wet is not only unpleasant, it can affect concentration, reaction times and use of the controls.

Speed:

- Ride at the correct speed to observe and deal with hazards in plenty of time.
- Ride at a speed so that you can pull up safely in the distance you can see to be clear and stay on your own side of the road.
- 'Only a fool breaks the two second rule' (double it in the wet).
- Not too fast - 30mph is a limit, not a target (e.g. outside schools).
- Not so slow as to cause frustration in other road users.
- Ride within your own limits which will increase with experience.
- Speeding fines can be very expensive and remember the six points maximum under the New Drivers Act.

Highway Code: (show it!)

This is an important and frequently underused document of value to all road users of all types and experience. It costs less than a magazine and is often updated. Ask some sample questions: e.g. what is the traffic light sequence, what does a 'Give Way' sign look like.

Anticipation:

- Look well ahead to give yourself time to deal with a hazard.
- Act before the situation gets out of control.
- Leave a safe gap (the two second rule) between yourself and the vehicle in front.
- Car drivers will not always signal when carrying out a U-turn.
- Develop a 'what if?' attitude.
- Expect a green light to turn to red.
- Watch out for bends tightening.
- Be able to stop (on your own side of the road) within your range of vision.
- A wet surface will offer a lot less grip.

Rear Observation:

- Important to know what might be coming up behind.
- Combine the use of mirrors and turning your head.
- Needed when:
- moving off
- turning
- overtaking
- changing speed
- Rear observation also gives a warning of your intentions.
- Don't rely on mirrors alone. Use the 180 degree checks and lifesavers.
- Don't look around too often, for too long or too late.
- Don't veer off course or wobble.

Road Positioning:

- Take up correct positions as often as you can.
- When travelling ahead this is usually in the centre of your own lane (dominant).
- Don't ride in the gutter or on the crown (take up the dominant position).
- Without swerving at the last second avoid potholes, spillages, debris and obstructions.
- Move slightly from the dominant position if it will assist other road users to see you, such as at junctions but revert to the dominant position once the hazard is passed.
- Don't ride in another vehicle's blind spot and watch out for a trailer cutting a corner.
- Keep to the nearside lane on dual carriageways.
- Consider and adapt your road position to maximise safety.
- It is easier for a motorcyclist to change their position to achieve a better view than it is for another road user.

Separation Distance:

Leave a safe space behind the vehicle you are following to allow you to pull up safely. Hanging back will also give a better view around the vehicle ahead.

Stopping distance equals thinking time plus braking time.

30mph: 9 metres + 14 metres = 23 metres
30mph: 30 feet + 45 feet = 75 feet

- 'Only a fool breaks the two second rule' (double in the wet).
- Always be able to stop in the distance that you can see to be clear.
- Cars with ABS can stop very quickly in the wet!
- In traffic, leave nearly a bike's length between yourself and the vehicle in front. When passing a parked vehicle, leave a door width's gap.

Weather conditions:

- Motorcyclists are badly affected by rain, cold, snow, ice, fog and wind.
- Always wear the best clothing you can afford no matter how short the journey or how hot the weather is.
- Keep your visor or goggles in the best condition for clearest vision and to minimise fogging.
- Make yourself visible to other road users.
- Extra stopping distance will often be required so consider reducing speed.
- Beware of strong winds on bridges and gaps between trees. Discuss the 'bow wave' effect when passing large commercial vehicles.
- In the snow and ice, postpone your journey. If in doubt, don't use the motorcycle.
- Discuss problems caused by a low sun.

Road surfaces:

Very important for motorcyclists in view of the small tyre contact area. Surface hazards include:

- mud
- leaves
- litter
- gravel
- loose road chippings
- potholes
- uneven surfaces
- inspection covers, especially when wet
- fuel spillages on bends, roundabouts, bus stops and petrol stations
- overbanding, also known as tarbanding
- painted areas
- polished or worn areas at junctions and roundabouts
- cats eyes
- tram lines

Road surfaces can become greasy when the first rain for some time falls after a long spell of hot and dry weather. Deal with such surface hazards in good time by looking and planning ahead so that you can avoid them without swerving suddenly. Special care will therefore be needed when accelerating, braking and cornering. Car drivers are unaware of our vulnerability to road conditions.

Alcohol and Drugs:

They impair our judgement, balance, concentration and reaction times.

80 milligrams per 100 millilitres of blood is the legal limit for alcohol. It is almost impossible to be sure if you are over or under the limit so don't drink and drive. Be aware of the risk of a potentially high reading the morning after a heavy drinking session.

Legally banned drugs also cause impairment of your senses.

With medicines, check with your doctor, pharmacist or the packaging as to whether or not it is OK to 'operate machinery'.

Quite apart from the increased risk of an accident, a conviction will result in serious consequences such as a ban with a large fine and very expensive insurance.

Attitude:

- A good attitude towards road safety is vital.
- Behave calmly, responsibly and patiently.
- Ride defensively and take nothing for granted.
- Keep concentrating and anticipating and be a good ambassador for motorcycling.
- Anger and competition will lead to mistakes and accidents.
- Despite provocation, don't react, retaliate or become involved in or fuel the spiral of 'road rage'.

Hazard Perception:

- A hazard is anything that is a potential risk. It is something that could cause us to change our speed or position. It is important to look as far ahead as possible and recognise hazards such as pedestrian crossings, children, loose dogs, horses and all other road users.
- Early recognition gives you more time to deal with hazards.
- Watch out for any vehicle movement clues such as an exhaust cloud or a reversing light on.
- Plan ahead and allow extra room.
- If a hazard crops up suddenly, reduce speed, look for an escape route and avoid 'target fixation'.
- Use all your senses, not just sight but also smell (diesel) and hearing (emergency sirens).
- Adjust your speed for a potential hazard. Can you stop safely in time?
- Your safety is in your control and the better your control, the safer you will be.

Element E - Practical on-road riding

Traffic lights: Remember the sequence and adjust your speed of approach. Watch out for any cyclist stop lines. Is the exit clear? Be aware of filter lights. If traffic lights have failed, proceed with caution, treating them as an unmarked junction where nobody has priority.

Roundabouts: Discuss the correct procedure aided by diagrams. Discuss the 'bail-out' procedure, i.e. the right indicator back on and go around the roundabout again. Lifesavers will be required. Explain the exit numbering system. A right turn is anything past the 12 o'clock position. Apply the OSM PSL procedure, adjusting your speed to hopefully filter in after first assessing the speed of other vehicles. Avoid misleading signals.

Junctions: Use observations to be aware of layout, road signs, markings and any hazards. Stop or give way? Initially, the instructor may make the decision. The OSM, PSL routine should be practised. Be aware that in the wet, the area close to the Give Way or Stop line may be more slippery than normal. When pulling up behind another vehicle, leave a gap of approximately one bike length.

Pedestrian Crossings: Pay special attention and be prepared to adjust your speed. Don't stop on a crossing causing a pedestrian's path to be blocked. Do not overtake on the zig-zag approach. Do not wave pedestrians across.

Gradients: On a hill start, use the rear brake like a car handbrake and use more accelerator. Avoid stalling and rolling backwards. On descents, adjust speed with the accelerator and brakes and then select the correct speed for that gear. Match gears to speed and load on ascent. Look out for warning signs on the approach to a gradient.

Bends: Always travel at a speed that allows you to stop safely in the distance you can see to be clear and stay on your own side of the road. Check for bad road surfaces, manhole covers, debris and cambers. Adjust your speed before entering the bend. Do not brake or change gear when the machine is leaning over.

Obstructions: Look well ahead (OSM, PSL) and move into position early. If the obstruction is on your side you must give way.

U-turn: Use the skill developed on the training pad as it is useful practice for the module one practical motorcycle test. It must be done at a safe location on a public road.

Emergency stop: This is also part of the module one practical motorcycle test. Reinforce the 'ABC' procedure. The student must react quickly to your signal (right arm extended vertically, slowly). If one tyre should skid, release and re-apply the brake with slightly less force. Ensure that the student doesn't snatch at the controls but uses them smoothly, firmly and progressively. In a genuine emergency there is not usually time for rear observations or gear changing. Explain to the student beforehand your procedure for alerting to them if you decide to abort a particular emergency stop.

Instructor on-road Notes:

Use the 'Keep It Short and Simple' (KISS) principle to give directions as the trainee will be nervous and in risk of brain overload. i.e. 'At the end of the road, turn left'. 'At the next roundabout, follow the road straight ahead'. 'Take the next road on the right'. Tell the student to continue going straight ahead (subject to traffic lights and signs!) until instructed otherwise to deviate. Alert-Direct-Identify. e.g. 'At the roundabout take the first exit, sign-posted Newtown'.

When organising the radio equipment don't rush or the ride will be frustrating for both student and instructor. Ensure all is correctly fitted and working at the correct volume with sufficient length of flex for rear observations.

Explain your radio procedure to the student. The student should nod the head if instructions are understood and they must shake the head if there is a problem. With voice-activated (VOX) equipment, start each instruction with '*Hello* ....' to switch it on and then speak without pause giving warning of where you plan for the student to go at the next junction. The instructions should be short and unambiguous. i.e. '*Follow the road straight ahead at the roundabout*' and not '*Go straight over the roundabout.*' To begin with give advance warnings, instructions and encouragement. As the student's confidence builds, it may not be necessary to use the radio quite as much. Only use the word '*right*' in the context of direction-giving rather than confirmation of something being correct. Avoid double negatives such as '*don't stop*'. Ask them instead to '*ride on*'.

Positioning: When pulling over for a debrief, remember not to pull in too close behind the student's machine when stopping as you need to ensure that when pulling away, you do not obscure the student's view of the road behind. If necessary, pull in ahead of the student. Your own positioning needs to be such that you have a good view of the student and the road ahead without causing any impairment of the student's vision.

As an alternative to the common system of having the instructor between two students, consider positioning yourself with both students ahead of you as this gives a better view of both of them. It is most important that the instructor has sufficient control of the students. The instructor must also have visual and radio contact at all times. At the very beginning of the road ride, seriously consider asking students to stop at the first few 'Give Way' junctions asking them to wait until you can position yourselves along side them so that you can check their view and decision-making when deciding to pull out. Once the first rider has emerged safely, maintain your own position so that the second student can ease forward to make their decision.

Lost or separated: Don't allow the students to become too stretched out, maintaining visual and radio contact at all times. If it happens, instruct the student to pull up on the left at the next available safe, convenient and legal place and to wait there until the instructor locates the student. If the solitary student has not been located within 15 minutes, they should make their own way directly back to the training school.

Frequent stops will be made to discuss situations and weaknesses, and to suggest remedies and prevent tiredness. Special allowance will have to be made for the effects of the weather upon the students. Lastly, double-check that the radio functions and watch the trainee through the 'FIGS' procedure and then adopt the safety position. All headlamps should be on dipped beam and safety vests should be worn and helmets correctly fastened.

As the road ride progresses and the student's confidence builds up, the instructor should gradually **reduce the amount of radio control** but be ready to quickly re-introduce it if it looks like the student needs it. 'Spoon feeding' is usually necessary at the outset with plenty of encouragement but it should be gradually reduced as the student appears to be improving. During the second half of the road ride the instructor needs to see that the student is coping competently and consistently with a variety of every day traffic situations with minimal prompting or warnings over the radio. Before issuing a DL196, the instructor should be satisfied that the student has displayed sufficient knowledge, skill and confidence to cope with every day traffic unsupervised.

When handing over the certificate I like to thank them for their hard work but stress that the certificate does not mean that they are a good rider, merely that they are good enough to continue the learning process on public roads under their own supervision.

I remind them that the DL196 is an important part of their driving licence which must be kept safe and I stress that as a learner rider they must display 'L' plates front and rear, they must not use motorways or carry pillion passengers, and they are restricted to riding nothing larger than a 125cc. (If they are 16 years old I explain that they are limited to a moped until their 17th birthday).

When reminding the student about the two year lifespan of the DL196, I suggest that this is more than adequate time in which to build up their experience, take additional training, and pass the theory and practical tests to avoid the need to re-take CBT in two year's time.

Chapter 10

Direct Access Scheme (DAS)

Once you have achieved your CBT1C card and gained a little more experience and guidance from more experienced instructors, the next stage is to become qualified to instruct students on larger machines (i.e. machines producing more than 47bhp). I attended Cardington in January 2004 for my Direct Access assessment. Fortunately I passed and here is a summary of my experiences. The Direct Access assessments take up only half a day on a one-to-one basis with the Cardington assessor in the role of a student motorcyclist. The candidate only ever plays the role of an instructor. When you first meet the assessor he will start off by outlining the agenda and precisely what is expected. In particular, he will tell you what pre-set tests you will be dealing with on the road ride. One therefore knows in advance precisely what scenarios you will have to deal with and there is also some time for preparation. You are, of course, allowed to refer to your notes and reference material which can also be used to instruct the 'student'.

The first part (theory) takes about 15 minutes and involves the candidate explaining the controls and differences between a 125cc learner machine and a large, powerful machine. Before you start, the assessor will outline any special features of the demonstration machine so that you can prepare for your briefing. For safety reasons, you are not required to manhandle the DSA's demonstration machine, which in my case was a Honda Varadero. It is important to emphasise the difference in power, weight, performance and braking.

The second part (on-site handling, approximately 30 minutes) takes place out on the 'pad' where the assessor plays the role of a student who has passed his CBT, bought a large machine and is having trouble in two aspects of its control. In my case it was slow speed manoeuvring and using the front brake smoothly to avoid excessive diving. In much the some way as one would do with a CBT student, I went through an explanation of what was required to improve matters

69

and I then worked the 'student' hard at practising these manoeuvres for himself.

On the braking exercise, my task was complicated slightly as the Varadero had linked brakes and firm application of the rear brake on its own caused quite a lot of front fork dive. The Honda also had handguards fitted which obscured my view of how the assessor was using the control levers. On reflection, perhaps I should have positioned myself differently so that I could observe him applying the brakes just as he came past me. In the final debrief, no comment was made by the assessor on this so I guess it was OK.

There is a 30 minute break before the final session involving road work, taking a total of 90 minutes. You will already have been given notice of three pre-set tests (out of a possible nine). My three tests were roundabouts, left/right turns and country roads and bends with 30 minutes for each test. In my case the 'student' was post-CBT and familiar with his large machine. The candidate is expected to correct any riding faults in the same way as one might on a CBT road ride. I chose to start each session with a talk with the 'student' to remind him of his CBT training, using lots of questions and answers to establish and refresh his knowledge.

On the faster, clearer sections of out-of-town roads you will be expected to keep up with the assessor and keep him under strict control if he looks like he is breaking any speed limits or is travelling too fast (for a novice) on approach to bends for example. You are, of course, expected to keep the required separation distance and ensure that your position minimises any obstructions of the 'student's' view.

My day concluded with a 10 minute debrief back at Cardington. My assessor suggested that I use the radio even more to give immediate correction of faults rather than frequent road-side debriefings but it was not a major criticism. He fully accepted that if one's radio was not of the highest quality then reduced dependence on same would be OK. As with the Cardington CBT assessment, marks are given on each element ranging from 1 to 4 with '4' being the highest mark and '3' being satisfactory.

Chapter 11

DAS and A2 lessons

Here is a list (not exhaustive) of topics that I like to cover on a DAS (Direct Access Scheme) or A2 course. They are in addition to topics that will have arisen on CBT which may need refreshing on a DAS or A2 course.

Angle start: The 'angle start' is a specific manoeuvre which crops up on the practical test, module two. When the student is asked to pull up behind a specific vehicle, they will need to allow sufficient space so that they can move off (after effective observations) around the parked vehicle. This is a test of their slow-speed balance and control. They should give a door width's gap and should not cause any other road users to change position or speed. Once students are comfortable with both hill and angle starts, I often combine the two, something which is unlikely to crop up on test.

Bends: Tell the student to evaluate the severity of the bend in plenty of time and use accelerator and brakes to adjust speed whilst the machine is still upright, before entering the bend. Set the speed for the bend on approach, then select the correct gear for the speed. Avoid braking and gear changing whilst the machine is leant over. The student should ensure that they are travelling at such a speed that they can pull up safely in the distance they can see to be clear and stay on their own side of the road.

Adopt the dominant position on approach and through the bend, assuming the dominant path offers satisfactory grip. On tight right hand bends with restricted visibility, it is in order to position the machine slightly to the left of the dominant position if this will give a better view of potential hazards ahead. This is not recommended if there is a drive or junction to the left where an emerging driver's view of yourself is reduced by your movement to the left of the dominant position. In addition, be wary of moving to the left of the dominant position if it could be interpreted by a following driver as an invitation for them to overtake. On left hand bends with restricted visibility, do not move to the right of the dominant line as this places the rider closer to oncoming traffic which might be cutting the corner.

Enter the bend on a 'trailing' or 'positive' accelerator, i.e. the accelerator is just open (slack taken up) as the machine will be more stable compared with being completely shut off on the overrun. Counter-steering could be discussed. Once the apex of the bend has been reached and you can see that the exit is clear, smoothly and gradually ease the accelerator open to gradually and progressively pick up speed as the machine becomes more upright. Continue with the dominant line and be aware of the implications of any camber and any factors which could affect grip.

Collision avoidance:

When I teach collision avoidance I stress that as soon as the serious hazard has been observed, the first priority is to reduce speed via the accelerator and then apply as much braking as safely possible, whilst the machine is still upright, before following an 'escape route' around the hazard, should one be available. It is important to scrub off as much speed as possible whilst upright so that any impact will be at a lower speed and also a last minute swerve will be more controllable. Quite often the serious hazard will be a car emerging from a side road in which case the rider needs to look for a big enough gap either side of the car and keep on looking into the gap as the bike will go where the rider is looking. If there is no escape route then the rider needs to focus upon a relatively 'soft' part of the car such as the centre of a door rather than a door pillar.

Emergency vehicles:

Keep a good look out not just for the emergency vehicle(s) but also any over-reaction (particularly sudden braking) from other road users. Be aware that once one emergency vehicle has passed, one or two more may follow. Look for a safe place to pull over to the left and until then maintain a safe legal speed. Try to choose a place to pull in where there will be sufficient space for the emergency vehicle to overtake easily without it having to lose too much speed. You are not exempted from road traffic law in your attempts to allow the emergency vehicle to pass.

Filtering:

This is a potentially hazardous operation which should only be carried out with great care and at a slow (less than 15mph) speed whilst overtaken vehicles are stationary or at least, stopping and starting very slowly. Remember the Highway Code instructions concerning overtaking. Watch out for pedestrians, car doors opening suddenly, 'cat's eyes', road users emerging from side-turnings and cyclists or motorcyclists also filtering. The overtaken vehicle may suddenly execute a U-turn without first checking or signalling.

Other road users and pedestrians are unlikely to be looking for motorcyclists. Consider 'risk and reward'. The risk of an accident is very high and the potential benefit (saving a few seconds on your journey time) is minimal. When nearing the front of a stationary queue, avoid creating a 'third lane' and instead, move back into one of the lanes courteously after a lifesaver and possible signal, avoiding 'cutting in'.

If another motorcyclist catches up with you when filtering, at the first safe opportunity, allow the other rider to go past. Do not overtake a filtering motorcyclist. Filtering is most dangerous when performed down the left side of the vehicles, between the traffic queue and the kerb. This is when you need to be vigilant for opening car doors, kerb drains and pedestrians stepping out. Avoid filtering on the left altogether if the traffic is moving. With two lines of stationary vehicles, the easiest course is usually between the two lines. You should flow back into one or other of the traffic lines as soon as the vehicles start moving freely again.

When filtering, watch for gaps developing, as that is when other road users are likely to switch lanes without warning. When filtering, you should always have a safe gap or space to take refuge in if a very wide, opposing vehicle approaches. Be aware though that such a gap opposite a junction or drive may also be large enough for a vehicle to emerge from.

Extra caution is required when filtering near junctions, especially on multi-lane roads and motorways. Vehicles joining or leaving can swap lanes with no warning when they are close to the junction. Do not cross a solid white line to filter past slow or stopped traffic.

Zig-zag markings on the approach to a pedestrian crossing mean you must not overtake the moving vehicle nearest to the crossing, nor must you pass the leading stationary vehicle on the crossing, unless it is stopped for a reason other than to allow pedestrians to cross. Great care is needed here, as pedestrians may not see you filtering through the stationary traffic.

Indicators:

Use with care and discretion. If in doubt apply these three tests.

1. Is it necessary?
2. Is it misleading?
3. Is there anyone to see it and benefit from it? (This includes pedestrians and cyclists).

There is no need to use them on giratory or one-way systems when you are already in the correct lane and are simply following its course. An exception to this rule is when you are on a roundabout with lane markings for specific routes. Discuss other methods of giving warnings - brake lights, arm signals, positioning, horn, headlamp. We are trying to make ourselves as predictable as possible to other road users.

Mirrors:

Use frequently to be updated on the situation behind. At minimum they should be used before slowing down and when changing speed and/or position significantly. When accelerating significantly (e.g. moving from a 30mph area to a 50mph area) on a single carriageway, a right lifesaver is usually a good idea, looking out for an overtaking vehicle in your blind spot. Like lifesavers, the mirror checks need to be effective, i.e. it is worth taking an extra mirror check to satisfy yourself that any following vehicles have reacted safely to your proposed manoeuvre.

Moving off in traffic:

When proceeding straight ahead in traffic and/or at traffic lights, consider a lifesaver glance into whichever side of you may have enough room for another road user who may be approaching from behind at a higher speed.

Overtaking:

Use OSM routine and observe road conditions and markings, remembering the Highway Code information on this topic. Give overtaken and approaching road users plenty of room and avoid 'cutting in' and causing other road users to change speed or position.

When waiting to overtake, keep at least a two second gap (in the dry). In particular, watch out for blind corners, hidden drives or road access points from which other road users might emerge. Look out for anything which might cause the overtaken vehicle to move into your path during your overtaking manoeuvre.

Make sure that you have the correct gear selected for responsive acceleration once the opportunity arises. Ideally, the rider should be able to reduce his speed if necessary at the end of the overtake solely by good accelerator control. Remember the 'risk and reward' principle.

Roundabouts:

Observe road signs on approach and adopt the correct lane for your destination. Adjust your speed to that of other traffic already on the roundabout so that you can enter the roundabout smoothly. On roundabouts with two lanes or more, take care to maintain a 'dominant' position within your lane on the approach, through the roundabout and upon your exit. Any exit past 12 o'clock on the roundabout sign should be treated as a right turn. Unless road signs and markings dictate otherwise, use the left lane for a left turn and straight ahead, right lane for a right turn.

When entering a roundabout consider whether or not road users entering the same roundabout from the 9 o'clock position will have had sufficient opportunity to observe your approach. Whilst proceeding around the roundabout, be aware of other road users approaching from your left in case they fail to give way.

Remember left lifesaver followed by left indicator just before you start to leave the roundabout on a right turn. On larger multi-lane roundabouts endeavour to take an extra lifesaver on the way in (into which ever lane you are not occupying) and another one on the way out (over the right shoulder) watching out for other road users entering or exiting at the same time as you.

Mini-roundabouts:

There is no requirement to indicate left as you exit as there is not usually sufficient time or space for a such a signal to be used helpfully. Use indicators as if you are approaching a crossroads. There is no need to indicate at all if you are following the road straight ahead via the second exit. If the straight ahead exit is being taken and it is the first exit, consider giving a left indicator on approach if it is not misleading.

Safety bubble:

Avoiding collisions with other road users, in the most basic of terms, is just about their proximity. If you can always maintain sufficient space then a collision will not occur. If you have sufficient space then you will also have enough time to see and deal with a hazard. I am not just talking about following distance but the concept of the 'safety bubble' as often mentioned by police riders. Think of it as an area of personal space all around your motorcycle extending out by a metre or so. You will not feel comfortable if another road user enters your 'safety bubble' as, at the very least, they have taken away any room for error.

Speed humps:

For continuous-width speed humps then they should be spotted early with good forward observation. Where necessary, reduce speed gradually after first checking in mirrors and maintain dominant position, with the machine vertical. If the humps have been spotted late and braking has been necessary, ensure that the front brake is released before the front wheel rides over the hump so that the front suspension has had time to settle back to its normal ride position before the hump is encountered. If the humps have gaps, then provided it is safe to do so, ride the motorcycle through the gaps. Good forward observation should mean that any change of position that may be necessary can be made gradually to avoid any last-minute swerving. When deciding which gap to pass through, consider the position of any parked or approaching vehicles as well as any bend in the road and the position of any nearby side roads. For example, will the change of position to pass through a gap place you unnecessarily close to other vehicles or cause you or other road users to have restricted visibility as a result? If you change position enough (approximately a metre or more) to require a check of the blind spot, then do one.

Steering:

Consider counterbalancing on U-turns and explain the principle of counter-steering. Keep the arms relaxed and avoid gripping the handlebars too tight. Keep the student's head up and look ahead early as the machine will go where the rider looks.

Chapter 12

Practical test preparation

For the student to be 'test-ready' they must not only have sufficient skills and knowledge but they must also believe that they have sufficient skills and knowledge. A positive mental attitude must be deployed where the student is encouraged to say (and think) that they can do this, not that they can't. They must be reminded about visualising some recent, good quality riding ensuring that when talking about previous problems, they are described in the past tense as something that has now been fixed.

For students who are very nervous, use '7-11' deep, slow breathing techniques to calm the nerves by encouraging extra oxygen flow to the brain. Take seven seconds to breathe in slowly through the nose and eleven seconds out through the mouth, to be done ten times. This has a physiological effect by providing more oxygen to the brain and will help to regain composure by altering certain chemical balances. It is an effective technique widely taught and is useful whether you are a soldier about to go into combat or a concert pianist about to perform before a large audience. Another method is through muscle relaxing. Starting at your feet, tense the muscles for fives seconds and then release. Repeat the process working your way up the body.

Why do tests make people nervous? It is an inescapable fact of life that exams and tests make people nervous but why does it so often cause an impairment of performance? What, if anything, can an instructor do to put the student at ease? I am a motorcycle instructor, not a psychologist. However, even I know that a little nervousness can be a good thing in stressful situations. Adrenalin is caused to flow, thereby raising our physical and mental faculties slightly. This makes sense when we reflect upon our primitive beginnings as a hunter and in particular, when we were being hunted. We should not be surprised that thousands of years later these basic bodily processes still happen but it seems to me that this type of reaction more often hinders than helps.

I regularly train policemen and women and I am often surprised at how worried some of them are about the motorcycle test, considering the variety of difficult situations that they routinely encounter in their work. One policeman told me how the previous week he had been called to a bank raid where it was known that the perpetrators were armed. Obviously a stressful situation, no matter how good the training. He told me that he found going to the raid less nerve-racking than taking his practical motorcycle test! How can that be? The medical profession call this 'performance anxiety'.

Another important factor is that the student should be in a positive frame of mind with the self-belief that the motorcycle test is a straightforward set of situations that they have already dealt with, to a good standard, during their training course. I often tell a nervous student that whilst everyone wants to pass first time, it doesn't always happen and there is no shame in taking the test a second time if things do not go well on the day.

Although it is usually too late by the time I first meet my student, I recommend that they keep to a minimum the number of people that know about their test. This will hopefully reduce the embarrassment of having to explain (and possibly re-live) the disappointment should they fail and, indirectly, reduce the pressure of passing.

Mock tests are very useful to give the student a realistic insight into the practical test but no matter how gruelling you make it, the student knows it is not the 'real thing'. It does however, put them under a little more pressure to perform to test standard and raises their concentration levels. To make it more realistic, one could always ask a fellow instructor (one that the student has not met before) to conduct such a 'test'. Using the army principle of 'train hard, fight easy', I always make the mock test slightly longer and more difficult than the real thing so that at it's conclusion, the student's confidence and self-belief is raised with the certain knowledge that there is nothing in the 'real' test to fear.

As a routine part of my training, I will have previously discussed with the student the format of the test so that they know exactly what to expect and what to do. No matter how short the training course may have been or how late in the day the test is scheduled, I always aim to have the student ready for test by the end of the previous training session. Attempting to include any last-minute tuition of new topics on the day is, I believe, unwise, as the student will often not be in the most receptive state to take on new information. I prefer it if the student has a simple ride over familiar territory to put themselves at ease on the machine.

I like to arrive at least ten minutes before test time to avoid any last minute rush. This is the most nerve-wracking time for the student. They will feel better once they are on their machine and they have completed their first manoeuvre. Talk about anything but the test. Ask them about their job, family, holidays or something that you know they enjoy doing and are able to talk about enthusiastically. Ask them to turn off their mobile phone.

The student should be asked to listen carefully to the examiner's directions and if it helps, say them back over to themselves, out loud, particularly on the module two test. This should help them to focus on the immediate task. The student should try to avoid rushing into implementing the examiner's instruction until they have allowed themselves a moment to plan how they will accomplish the instruction. For example: before switching on the indicators, the student should take a second to look at the layout of the junction to ensure that any indication given is not misleading. I remind the student that they should not think about something that has happened previously. This will only distract them from their next manoeuvre. If they think they have made a mistake, they should assume it is a 'minor' and not dwell on it.

As with so many things in life, you never stop learning. The most interesting part of my job is meeting a wide variety of people from all sorts of backgrounds. I think it is important to quickly build up a rapport so that you can understand, as soon as possible, how exactly you will need to adapt your teaching approach to best suit your student. The human psyche is a complex device. Pity it doesn't come with an instruction manual!

Chapter 13

Practical test preparation module one manoeuvres

Once the student has developed sufficient skill and confidence they are ready for their practical tests. Students find it quite helpful to have visited the test centre and its environs during training but avoid parking in a DSA test centre car park until the day of the test and even then, try not to arrive more than ten minutes before the allotted time.

Before you set off, make sure that the student has all of their documents (CBT and theory certificates, together with photo card licence and paper counterpart). If the address on the student's licence is incorrect, ask them to write in the necessary changes on the relevant section of the counterpart before the test starts. Once the module one test has been passed there will be the pass certificate to present in addition when taking module two. Before leaving base, check that the machine to be used is reasonably clean and presentable with horn and all lights working, valid tax disc and 'L' plates correctly displayed, plus plenty of fuel.

There will be a specific motorcycle parking area for students on test. Space is usually at a premium so the instructor's machine should be parked elsewhere. I recommend that the test machine be parked on its centre stand facing outwards ready for an easy exit. Make sure the keys are removed, indicators cancelled and the headlamp switch is in the 'on' position. Even the most competent of students will be nervous so whilst passing the time before test, engage them in conversation to hopefully take their mind off the imminent test.

I always ask the student's permission to watch their module one test and if they agree, I do it from a discreet distance. At the conclusion of either test, I ask for the student's consent (within the examiner's earshot) for me to listen to the debrief which is usually helpful. Once the student has left the room, don't be afraid to discuss topics with the DSA examiner so that you fully understand his debriefing. Try to get to know your local examiners and build up a rapport so that you can extend your knowledge and understanding of what they are looking for.

The current two-part motorcycle test came into effect on April 27th 2009 so I thought it would be useful to provide some detail. There are eleven elements to module one, which are carried out in the following order within the purpose-built MMA (Motorcycle Manoeuvring Area). It is important that the student carry out effective observations whilst inside the MMA. In other words, although there should not be any other vehicles (and only one pedestrian - the examiner) in the fenced off area, the student should still carry out effective observations as if they were on a public road. Fortunately the student does not have to memorise the procedure as the examiner will be on hand at each stage to describe what happens next. The examiner will open the enclosed MMA and ask the student to ride into, and then stop in, a box of four green cones.

module one manoeuvres

1. on and off the stand
2. wheel the machine
3. slalom
4. figure-of-eight
5. 30 kph / 19 mph circuit ride
6. 50 kph / 32 mph avoidance
7. controlled stop
8. U-turn
9. slow ride

10.   30 kph / 19 mph circuit ride

11.   50 kph / 32 mph emergency brake

1. The student must first park the motorcycle on either stand so that the machine is nose-first in a 'box' of four green cones representing a garage-sized space 2.5 metres wide.

2. The motorcycle must then be taken off the stand and pushed backwards in a wide semi-circle into another 'box' of four green cones. The conventional method is to be alongside the nearside of the machine with the left hand on the handlebar and push backward with the right hand gripping the seat or some convenient hand hold at the rear of the bike. The arc of the turn is very wide and, of course, the road surface is flat and offers good grip.

3. A slalom through five yellow cones must be executed. As they are spaced at 4.5 metre intervals, few students should find this difficult.

4. Following straight on from the slalom the rider must then immediately perform two consecutive figure-of-eight manoeuvres around two blue cones positioned (6 metres apart) at the end of the slalom.

5. Next is riding the machine through a curve (of 19 metre radius) following a long and wide line of red cones at at least 19mph but there is no measuring equipment used to check this. This immediately leads into:

6. The avoidance manoeuvre. As the student exits the curve sufficient acceleration must be applied so that the machine registers at least 32mph as it passes through the speed measuring device. The instant that the 1.5 metre wide speed trap has been passed through the student must make a swerve to pass through two blue offset cones. Once that has been done the next element follows on immediately.

7. Controlled stop. The machine should be brought to a stop with the front wheel coming to rest in the middle of a 'box' of four blue cones. It is 1.5 metres wide and 1 metre deep.

8. U-turn. Two white lines (denoting kerbs) are painted 7.5 metres apart so that a standard U-turn can be executed. This is easier than the old style test as there is no traffic, kerbs or cambers to deal with. The usual observations should be carried out.

9. The student must ride the machine at walking speed in a straight line for 17 metres between two pairs of green cones 3.1 metres apart.

10. The student must repeat number five (circuit ride) in the same direction as before and must pass through the speed trap and register at least 32mph.

11. Module one is concluded with a standard emergency stop. Whilst the approach speed (32mph required) is measured accurately, the distance or time taken to stop is not.

A maximum of five minor riding faults is allowed. Any more will result in a fail. The student needs to avoid touching any cones and putting their feet down during the slow speed manoeuvres. If the student has failed to achieve the necessary 32mph speed on either the avoidance or emergency stop manoeuvres then at the end of the test, they are allowed one more attempt at each to achieve the speed.

The only manoeuvre worthy of special attention is the **avoidance manoeuvre** (6). To make things a little easier for the student I recommend that they engage second gear well before the curve and then leave the machine in second gear all through the entire avoidance manoeuvre. Once the machine exits the curve it must be aimed between two red cones and then a 'box' of red and yellow cones containing the speed measuring device. These six cones create a passage just under 1.5 metres wide. The student must resist the temptation to close off the accelerator before the speed trap, as 10 metres beyond it the student must execute a swerve between two blue cones. Counter-steering would be a good idea here. At 32 mph the student is covering 14.3 metres per second and so there is just time (roughly two thirds of a second) to close the accelerator but not apply the brakes.

I encourage my students to break the manoeuvre down into four distinct phases:

1. Steady approach speed: once in second gear, maintain road speed through the curve with no further gear changes. When exiting the curve, look ahead and accelerate smoothly towards the speed trap 'corridor' of cones. The instant that the speed trap box is entered:

2. Shut the accelerator and then:

3. Apply some **steering** effort to move around the offset blue cone. Look ahead for the four blue cones comprising the 'stop-box' and with the accelerator still shut,

4. Apply the front **brake**, then rear brake.

Emergency Stops:

When practising on public roads, find a safe and quiet location with good visibility and surfaces where no irritation will be caused to local residents. Make sure you have explained your abort procedure at the outset. Once the emergency stop has been completed, encourage the student to take effective rear observation to observe any following traffic and then, with the clutch still held in, 'paddle' the machine towards the kerb 'out of harm's way'. Finally, select neutral or first gear. On larger machines, if the student finds it easier, then it is in order to select first gear and drive to the kerb side provided there is not too much delay. The priority is to have the machine moved out of harm's way speedily without the emergency stop being compromised.

Chapter 14

Practical test preparation module two (road ride)

Module two involves a road ride (approximately 35 minutes) without any special manoeuvres other than an angle and a hill start. Passing the module one test should confirm that the student has sufficient skill in the handling of the motorcycle itself and the road ride should show that this skill can be combined with interacting satisfactorily with the road system and other road users.

The majority of students will expect to be shown the area in which they will be tested and if there are any noteworthy junctions or situations then they should be shown them. I always like to stress that once a student has sufficient skill and knowledge then it should not matter where they are tested. In a perfect world they should be capable of riding to a good and safe standard in any town or city, without having been there before. The priority is to avoid excessive use of known test routes in the mistaken belief that this will improve the student's riding. It is important to avoid annoying local residents and getting in the way of other learners (car or motorcycle) taking their tests.

As with module one, arrive at the test centre ten minutes or so before the allotted test time having made sure before departure that the student has all five of the required documents. Most students will need at least an hour or so on the bike to get into their familiar routines. In very cold weather, it might be an idea to arrive at the test centre in plenty of time so that the student has the opportunity to warm up any cold extremities.

The examiner will start by checking the student's documents and he will then explain the test procedure. Radio equipment will be supplied and checked just before setting off. Before the ride starts there will be an eyesight test by reading a car number plate just over 20 metres away. This is followed by a couple of very straightforward machine maintenance-type questions which can be obtained from the DSA website.

Most of the time, the examiner follows the student on a motorcycle and sometimes in a car. In the latter event, I would strongly recommend that you ask permission to sit in the car to observe proceedings, particularly if you have not seen such a test before. If the examiner is using a motorcycle then ask permission to follow on your own machine. They should be happy to oblige.

The examiner is looking for a competent, safe and legal ride with appropriate consideration shown for other road users. It is important that the student does not cause another road user to change speed or position. The examiner will give clear and timely instructions over the radio as to the route that the student should follow and in the absence of any directions, the student should follow a straight ahead course.

If the examiner's directions are not clear, a shake of the student's head should cause the examiner to repeat them. If they become confused on a roundabout, they should not change their mind or route part way through. Instead, the student should take a safe and legal route consistent with their indications and positioning.

Emphasise to the student that they cannot incur even a 'minor' for taking a different route to the one asked provided it is done safely and legally. Following a precise test route is not actually part of the test and it is important to avoid over-familiarity with a particular route. Intelligent use of the indicators is important combined with swift cancellation to avoid the signal being misleading.

At the conclusion of either test, I ask for the student's consent (within the examiner's earshot) for me to listen to the debrief which is usually helpful. More than ten riding faults ('minors') would constitute a fail.

Chapter 15

Post test instructing

So far I have concentrated upon preparing motorcycle riders to achieve a full UK motorcycle licence but post-test training is just as important. Many riders have little difficulty in achieving the required standard to secure a full motorcycle licence but once passed many will slip into bad habits and some may become complacent, over-confident and develop a poor attitude towards road safety. From a professional motorcycle instructor's point of view, once CBT and Direct Access qualifications have been achieved, what is next in terms of securing a government-authorised, post-test instructing qualification? There was nothing until the December 2007 launch of the Enhanced Rider Scheme (ERS).

I must praise the DSA for introducing the splendid 'Enhanced Rider Scheme'. In simple terms, it is the motorcycling equivalent of the car world's 'Pass Plus'. The DSA has addressed an area that was due for regulation, namely, post-test motorcycle training. Until quite recently, there has been something of an anomaly in this area. It is this. In the UK there are many motorcycle trainers offering 'advanced' tuition to riders who already have full motorcycle licences but who would like to brush-up and enhance their riding skills. The trainers offering this service are usually very experienced and highly-motivated motorcyclists acting with the best of intentions. They are quite often former or serving police motorcyclists. There are also a number of umbrella organisations, each offering their own, self-regulated training possibilities. They include the Driving Instructor's Association, the Institute of Advanced Motorists and RoSPA (Royal Society for the Prevention of Accidents). It always seemed a little strange to me that the Government (via the DSA) quite properly regulated instructors providing pre-DSA test instruction but left post-test tuition to its own devices.

A curious irregularity that remains is that one can achieve an 'advanced' motorcycle instructor qualification without first securing qualifications to teach beginners. To the layman, this might appear to be illogical but in practical terms it rarely causes a problem. What might be confusing to Joe Public is being confronted with choosing between three organisations all offering 'advanced' training none of which are regulated by the government. Some of the organisations have even negotiated discounts with some motorcycle insurers once the client has achieved an 'advanced' standard.

As soon as it was announced, I decided that I wanted to join the DSA's Register of Post-test Motorcycle Trainers (RPMT). You will need to be on this register to provide ERS training. One of the conditions for joining the register is that one must pass the special theory test. Any instructor interested in joining should send off a small payment for the instructor information pack which includes a reference book of the theory test questions and answers, plus a DVD.

I congratulate the DSA on the use of the word 'enhanced' when naming this scheme. By deliberately not using the word 'advanced', it is opening it up to those riders who might otherwise have been put off, believing that 'advanced' training will require them to ride to a standard slightly beyond their experience, ability and inclination. The word 'enhanced' is much more inclusive and therefore it can be aimed at those riders whose machine-handling and road skills need to raised. Insurance discounts are available from a large number of insurance providers to those riders who have demonstrated a good standard of riding to the ERS instructor. There is no formal test for the student but instead there is a process of continuous assessment, ideally culminating in the instructor issuing a certificate which will entitle the student to an insurance discount. The DSA supplies a very good marketing pack to assist the ERS instructor with useful ideas on how to promote their services which will be of particular benefit to an instructor not attached to a DSA Approved Training Body. Copies of the rider appraisal forms need to be submitted to the DSA on a quarterly basis.

By virtue of my previous instructing experience (and being an early applicant) I was eligible to join the register via a 'grandfather' rights route, a condition of which was that I must be subjected to a check-test of my instructional ability within twelve months of joining the RPMT register. It was conducted at my local DSA test centre (at no charge) by the CBT manager for the area. He rang me about a week before the test to outline the format of the session and offer me a selection of nine pre-set tests, each one of which contains five topics where the 'student' needs to improve. The examiner will need your selection a few days in advance of the test date so that he can work out a suitable route. On the test day, he will tell you which student role he will play for all five elements. The check test itself takes at least an hour plus 15 minutes at either end for discussion. The check test is very similar to the road-ride element of the Cardington direct access assessment. As with DAS, the examiner may reproduce faults outside the scope of the five elements which you will have to spot and correct. The examiner will signal to you where he wants you to direct him using the DSA's radios. The only drawback is that whilst you know the 'student's' weaknesses at the outset, you cannot plan the lesson or the route and you have to teach and correct topics as they crop up. In my case, if I had been dealing with a 'real' student, I would have taken them to a safe and quiet area first to fix their slow-speed problems before working on junctions and roundabouts.

Chapter 16

Driving Standards Agency

From time to time, the DSA will send a representative (usually a CBT manager) to observe you conducting a CBT as they want to ensure that standards are being maintained. The CBT managers are looking for the core competencies of fault identification and analysis plus remedial action. Because they visit so many schools they see lots of good ideas and are therefore in a position to share best practice. Some instructors have a morbid fear of such visits as they are worried that their instructor card will be taken away. These fears are without foundation for competent instructors. The CBT manager just wants to see a normal CBT being carried out to the required standard, just as you normally do. Sometimes an instructor will be removed from the register if the instruction provided is dangerous to the public and they have failed to improve their standards following a previous, unsatisfactory observation. The easiest way to be removed from the register is failing to provide CBT students with the minimum of two hours on-road tuition (element E).

These visits are an ideal opportunity for observer and student to pick up and exchange ideas and generally improve. It is only human nature to be a little nervous, and to make sure that nothing important is missed out use notes or a crib sheet as a check list. If the CBT manager takes notes it doesn't mean that mistakes have been made. It is more likely that the start and finish times are being recorded along with maybe one or two discussion points. The CBT managers (in my experience) are approachable and happy to talk and answer questions but if preferred, they can also keep quiet and let the instructor crack on.

Unfortunately, there is a lot of mistrust of the DSA amongst some schools and instructors which does not help anyone. The vast majority of examiners and CBT managers that I have met have been very friendly and helpful. Whatever one's feelings about a particular DSA policy, as instructors we must work hard to have a good relationship with the various DSA officials that we have contact with. The CBT managers are more than happy to talk to instructors about any issues that crop up such as problems with particular examiners or developing training packages.

The most important thing to remember is that instructors and DSA employees should work together because they share the same objective, namely improving road safety.

CBT Section
The Axis Building
112 Upper Parliament Street
Nottingham
NG1 6LP
e-mail: cbt@dsa.gsi.gov.uk

Phone: 0115 936 6547
www.dsa.gov.uk

Chapter 17

Glossary

A2: A training course where the student rides a 125cc machine

ABC: Accelerator, Brakes and Clutch

ATB: Approved Training Body

BABS: Braking, Acceleration, Balance and Steering

BESTCOPS: Brakes, Electrics, Steering, Tyres, Chain, Oil, Petrol and Suspension

CBT: Compulsory Basic Training

CBT1: The certificate issued after an instructor has been successfully down-trained

COS: Cancel signal, Observation (rear) and Speed up

DL196: Certificate of completion of training

DIA: Driving Instructors Association

DSA: Driving Standards Agency

EDP: Explain, Demonstrate and practise

ERS: Enhanced Rider's Scheme

FIGS: Fuel, Ignition, Gears and Starter

IAM: Institute of Advanced Motorists

KISS: Keep It Short and Simple

LADA: Look, Assess, Decide, Act

MMA: Motorcycle Manoeuvring Area

OSM: Observation, Signal and Manoeuvre

POWDERY: Petrol, Oil, Water, Damage, Electrics, Rubber and 'You'!

POWER: Petrol, Oil, Water, Electrics and Rubber

PSL: Position, Speed, Look.

Q & A: Question and Answer

RoSPA: Royal Society for the Prevention of Accidents

RPMT: Register of Post-test Motorcycle Trainers

RTA: Road Traffic Accident

RTC: Road Traffic Collision

SCALP: Safe, Convenient And Legal Place.

Chapter 18 - Bibliography

Here is a recommended (but not exhaustive) reading list;

'The Official Highway Code' by the DSA. ISBN 978-0115528149

'Know Your Traffic Signs' by Department of Transport. ISBN 978-0115528552

'The Official DSA Guide to Learning to Ride' by the DSA. ISBN 978-0115526459

'The Official DSA Guide to Riding (the essential skills)' by the DSA. ISBN 978-0115526442

'Motorcycle Roadcraft' ISBN 978-0113411436

'How to be an Advanced Motorcyclist' by IAM. Published in 2004 ISBN 0 7603 2036 5

'The Assessment of Advanced Motorcycling' by Dave Jones. Published in 1998 ISBN 978-0952974710

'Not The Blue Book' by Dave Jones. Published in 1997 ISBN 978-0714038117

'Mind Driving' by Stephen Haley. Published in 2006 ISBN 978-1873371169

Printed in Great Britain
by Amazon